This book belongs to

_____

This book is dedicated to my children - Mikey, Kobe, and Jojo.

Ninja Life Hacks™

Sad Ninja

By Mary Nhin

Pictures by
Jelena Stupar

One evening, I laid awake in my bed. I was having a hard time falling asleep.

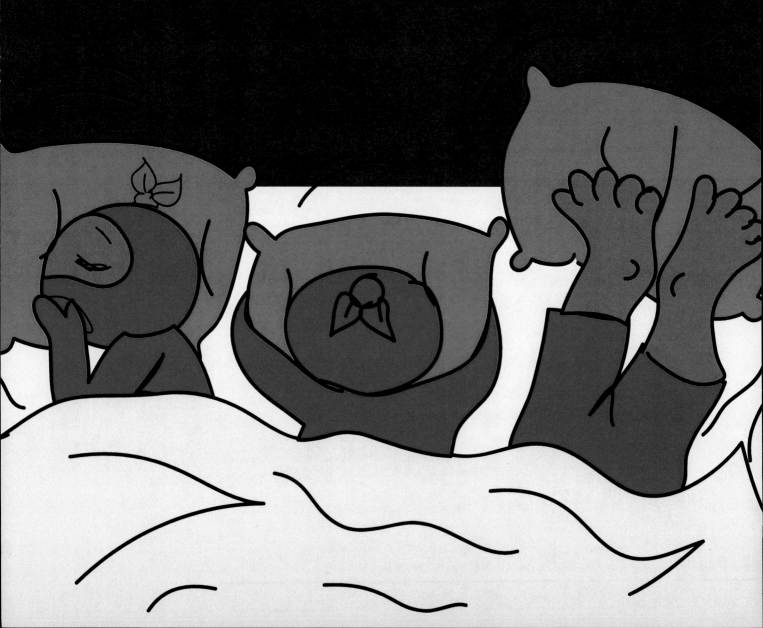

Lately, I had been worrying a lot. I learned my grandmother had just died. I was very close to my grandma.

It was a rough year and it affected me in all sorts of ways...

Sometimes, my head hurt and my stomach would tighten up.

I would often get mad.

Other times, I'd cry and didn't want to do anything.

Not even my favorite things...

One day, Lonely Ninja came to visit me.

You can use any or all of these tools:

Say goodbye.

Accept your feelings and talk about it.

Do something creative and active.

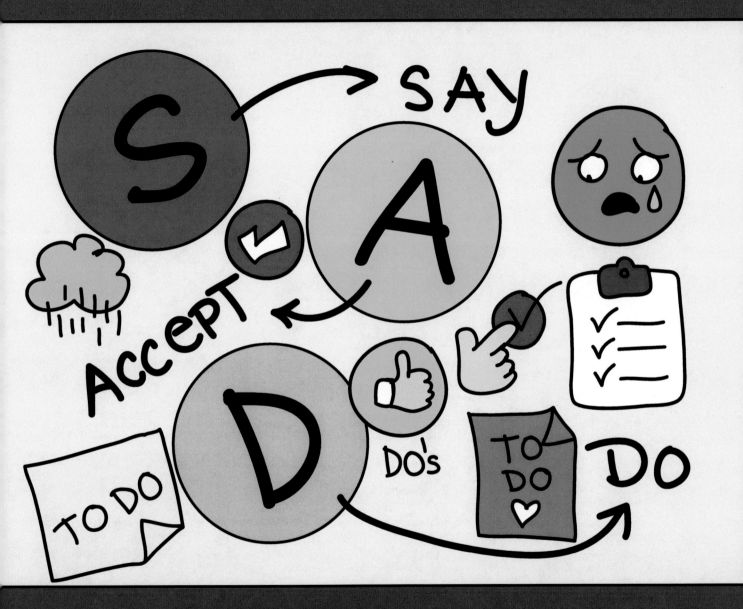

Say your goodbyes by making a memory journal or attending a funeral.

Accept your feelings and talk about it
with a parent, teacher, or counselor.

Do something creative and active everyday.

I went home later that night and told my dad about what I had learned about accepting sad feelings.

Say goodbye.

I decided I'd start with a memory journal. I filled it with memories of my grandmother and the fun times we shared. It made me smile to think about all those special moments.

Accept your feelings and talk about them with a parent, counselor, or teacher.

I didn't know how it happened, but after saying goodbye and talking about things, I was already feeling better.

So, I proceeded with the last thing Lonely Ninja mentioned in the S.A.D. strategy.

Do something creative and active.

I practiced my musical pieces and played basketball.

That evening, my spirits had lifted and I slept peacefully.

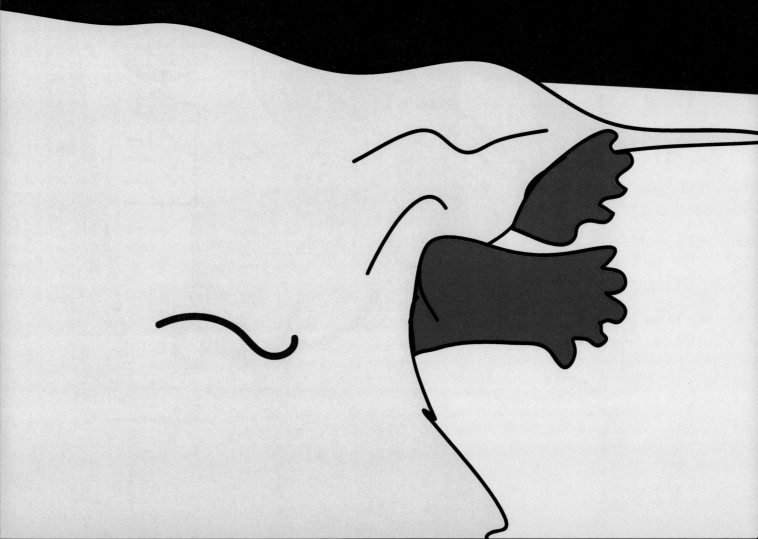

Remembering to use the S.A.D. strategy could be your secret weapon in dealing with sad feelings.

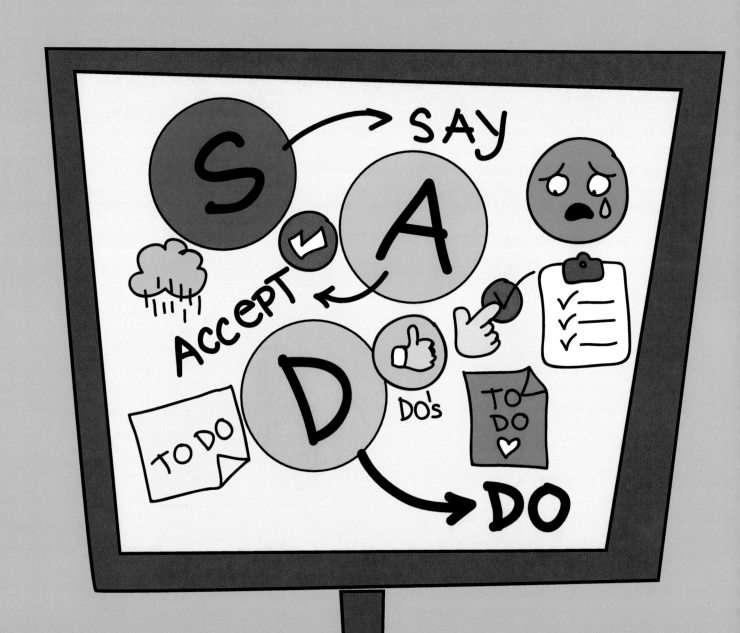

Please visit us at ninjalifehacks.tv to check out our box sets!

@marynhin   @GrowGrit
#NinjaLifeHacks

Mary Nhin   Ninja Life Hacks

Ninja Life Hacks

79012190R00021